THE DATING COMPATIBILITY TEST

THE DATING COMPATIBILITY TEST

Daniella Martina

CITADEL PRESS
Kensington Publishing Company
www.kensingtonbooks.com

CITADEL PRESS BOOKS are published by

Kensington Publishing Corp.
850 Third Avenue
New York, NY 10022

Copyright © 2001 by Daniella Martina

All rights reserved. No part of this book may be reproduced in any form or by any means without the prior written consent of the publisher, excepting brief quotes used in reviews.

All Kensington titles, imprints, and distributed lines are available at special quantity discounts for bulk purchases for sales promotions, premiums, fund-raising, educational, or institutional use. Special book excerpts or customized printings can also be created to fit specific needs. For details, write or phone the office of the Kensington special sales manager: Kensington Publishing Corp., 850 Third Avenue, New York, NY 10022, attn: Special Sales Department, phone 1-800-221-2647.

Citadel Press and the Citadel Logo are trademarks of Kensington Publishing Corp.

First printing: December 2001

10 9 8 7 6 5 4 3 2 1

Printed in the United States of America

Library of Congress Control Number: 2001094204

ISBN 0-8065-2292-5

Contents

Introduction	vii
Part I "You Say Potato, and I Say Potahto"—Personality Traits	1
1. Moods and Quirks	3
2. Physical Attraction	13
3. Character and Beliefs	21
4. Last Laughs—Sense of Humor	30
5. Tastes—Movies and Music	37
6. "Eat Drink Man Woman"—Food Questions	45
7. Mind and Intellect	54
8. Athletic Support	61
9. It's Just Money—or Is It?	68

10.	"In Dreams Begin Responsibilities"—Dreams and the Future	74
11.	The Basics	82

Part II "Where Do We Go From Here?"—The Dating Experience 85

12.	First Date	87
13.	Not Another Movie, Please!	95
14.	Sex	100
15.	Friends and Family	108
16.	Where Private Meets Public	114
17.	The Phone, the Internet, and Thou	120
18.	Saturday Night and Sunday Morning (and Weekend Trips)	129
19.	Fighting the Good Fight	137
20.	To Commit or Not to Commit	142
21.	Away Time	150
22.	"Where Were You?"—Suspicion, Jealousy, and Trust	155
23.	The Test Test	163

INTRODUCTION

In the era of Dating Services (*expensive*) and Personal Ads (*embarrassing*), it is nice to know that there is an inexpensive and respectable alternative to guide you through the wilds of the Dating Jungle. That alternative is this book—an exhaustive series of questions that will help you identify who's right for you.

I know this jungle well, believe me. I am a veteran dater, with experience in the small town where I went to high school and dated everyone from the captain of the basketball team to the pimply nerd who now runs his own brokerage firm; in college where, by actual count, I dated a total of twenty-two different men, none of whom felt remotely like Mr. Right; and in New York City where I now work, a city in which dating routinely varies from the heights of romantic bliss to the depths of meat-market humiliation. I have had my share of blissful nights and horrendous hurts, of exhilarating encounters and endlessly boring conversations, of hearty laughs and stifled yawns.

I think I am a fairly typical dater: fussy and romantic, impatient and cautious, fun-loving and serious, and (until very recently) always on the lookout for my perfect match. Happily, after somewhere in the vicinity of five hundred lifetime dates, I finally found that match and, dear reader, as this little book goes to press, I am sending out invitations for our wedding.

On my long and serpentine route to the altar, I think I have realized a great deal about what goes on in dating, what you can learn from it and how you can use that knowledge to make the mating game more enjoyable and less traumatic, more edifying and less tedious, and above all, a more efficient way to find out who is right for you.

I am one of those people who keeps a diary religiously—especially about my dates—so I have been able to draw on several handwritten volumes of dating history in preparing this book. In addition, I have been blessed throughout my life with good friends who have willingly shared their experiences. It is my hope and theirs that what follows will save you from some of the follies, dead ends, and just plain painful experiences that we endured.

The Dating Compatibility Test works effectively at four different levels.

> First: It helps you clarify in your own mind what kind of person and what kind of relationship you are looking for.

Second: By taking this test with someone else, you can determine if the two of you are potentially a good match.

Third: Taking this test with someone else is a terrific way to open up discussions of important topics that you may otherwise be reluctant to bring up.

Fourth: Taking this test either alone or with someone else is a great way to see relationships and dating issues from the other person's point of view. (You will really see this operating in Chapter 22, "'Where Were You?'—Suspicion, Jealousy, and Trust.)

Dating can provide you with some of the best times of your life. But with the wrong person, dating also can provide you with one of the biggest wastes of time in your life—time you could be spending finding someone much more suitable for you. So above all, these questions and your answers are a fabulous time saver.

A few thoughts about how to approach these questions. On the one hand, approach them honestly. *There are no right answers, just good matches*. It makes no sense to hedge your responses—let the truth ring out now and you can save yourself a lot of grief later. On the other hand, approach them playfully. Taking the test should be fun, not a chore. That may sound like a contradiction—*How can you be both honest and playful?* Easy. The fact is that you will come up with your most spontaneous and honest responses when you are having a good time.

One caveat: *Always leave one small part of yourself open to surprises and contradictions.* After answering these questions, you may discover that everything points to a doomed relationship with Person X—*I could never date a Republican divorcee who smokes cigars*—yet there is something about this Person X that makes your heart go pitter-pat anyhow. In that case, you just may want to go with your heart and not with the Compatibility Test.

But that said, what you have in your hands right now is an incredibly efficient and probing Do-It-Yourself Dating Service. I don't have a list of available singles in the back, but when you think about it, the hard part is not finding *someone* to date—it's finding the *right* person to date. And this book can go a long way in helping you find that person.

The Dating Compatibility Test is divided into two major sections. Part I, "You Say Potato, and I Say Potahto," is comprised of questions that pinpoint personality and character traits—your own and the traits you generally like and dislike in the people you date. Part II, "Where Do We Go from Here?" is comprised of questions that define your desires and expectations in the dating experience itself.

Okay, ready?
Go for it!

Part I
"You Say Potato, and I Say Potahto"—Personality Traits

A good match almost always means compatible personality traits—compatible moods, beliefs, senses of humor, values, and tastes. But *compatible* personality traits do not necessarily mean *matching* traits. Fact is, dating someone who is exactly like you in most respects can be a little on the boring side—like going out with a life-size mirror (albeit one with different anatomy).

Compatible traits are most often *complementary*—they go together without being precisely the same. Still, there are a great many traits that each person finds "off the charts"—you know that you simply could never develop a lasting relationship with someone who has them. For example, you may be pretty sure that someone who is shorter than you are or who hates Chinese food or who doesn't believe in God is not the person you want. It doesn't matter if someone else thinks these traits are trivial in the Grand Scheme of Things—they are important to *you*. And, in the final analysis, they can tell you a lot about who you should date and who you shouldn't.

1 Moods and Quirks

Moods are more than just passing feelings. If you stack together all of a person's daily moods, you pretty much end up with *who they are*. Likewise, someone's quirks of behavior are more than just those funny little things they do once in a while—they add up to how a person acts in general. So take a close look at the moods and quirks of a person you are considering dating. And just as importantly, take a good look at how this person reacts to your own Ps and Qs.

1. If you are in a bad mood, you want the person with you to

    a. ignore your mood.
    b. ask you what's wrong.
    c. keep you company by getting into a bad mood too.
    d. try to coax you out of your mood by telling jokes and singing funny songs.
    e. leave you alone.

2. If a person, early on in the relationship, confesses to being on Prozac, your reaction is:

   a. Telling me was a brave act of trust and I should respect it.
   b. How the hell do I know who this person *really* is?
   c. Maybe I can make this person so happy the pills won't be needed anymore.
   d. I'd better start easing myself out of this relationship pronto.

3. If your date excuses sullen behavior on three dates in a row by claiming to be "in a bad mood," you think:

   a. Poor baby, maybe I can help.
   b. I wonder if it's something about *me* that's causing this bad mood.
   c. Shape up or ship out, buddy.

4. If you notice that your date has a nose-tapping ritual—three times before crossing the street (*every* time), you think:

   a. That's kinda cute.

MOODS AND QUIRKS

    b. That's sick.

    c. Other: _____

5. If someone needs a full hour of silence to "become a person again," your reaction is:

    a. Don't be so bloody precious and self-indulgent.

    b. Hey, everyone's entitled to their little quirks.

6. If someone regularly talks back to the weather lady on TV, your reaction is:

    a. Isn't that cute.

    b. Let me out of here.

7. Nobody is perfect.

    True/False

8. If a person confesses, early on in the relationship, to being in psychotherapy, your reaction is:

    a. I wonder if they talk about me in the therapy sessions.

b. This person could change radically any day, so I better not get too attached.
   c. If this person has problems, why not talk about them with me instead of with a shrink?
   d. Who needs a person with so many heavy-duty problems that they need to see a shrink?
   e. No big deal.

9. A person who goes from joyful to sad and back again two or three times in a single evening is

   a. a person with an exciting range of emotions.
   b. a person with emotional problems.

10. A person who tells you three totally different and contradictory stories about their background on three different occasions is

    a. a person with an interesting imagination.
    b. a pathological liar who you'd better get rid of real quick.

MOODS AND QUIRKS

11. If someone you've recently begun seeing regularly arrives a half-hour late for dates, you

    a. let it pass; some people are just that way.
    b. say firmly but politely that you really don't appreciate that kind of treatment.
    c. stand them up the next time they're late.

12. If you notice that someone you have been seeing for a while is always talking about Big Plans, but never seems to get around to doing anything about them, you think:

    a. Hey, I'm that way, too.
    b. I'd rather be with a dreamer than with somebody who has no dreams at all.
    c. This person has a lot of growing up to do—and who's got the time?

13. If a person you have just begun seeing tells the same personal story on three different occasions, *each time as if it is being told to you for the first time*, your reaction is:

    a. Gosh, it doesn't take much to make someone feel nervous.

b. That's kinda cute.

c. Wonder how it's going to feel when I hear it for the three *hundredth* time? Let me out of here!

14. If a person gets to the middle of telling a joke and then says, "Gee, I forgot how the rest of it goes," you say:

    a. That's funny, that happens to me all the time, too.
    b. Maybe I can help you remember the rest of it.
    c. Maybe we can make up the rest of the joke together.
    d. Why the hell do you start telling a joke if you aren't sure you know how it ends?

15. Someone who routinely laughs loudest in telling a joke is

    a. self-assured.
    b. insecure.
    c. an idiot.

MOODS AND QUIRKS

16. If a person never looks you in the eye when talking to you, this means the person is probably

   a. very shy.
   b. madly attracted to you and afraid to show it.
   c. very sneaky.
   d. very bad mannered.

17. If a person you have just started seeing always touches you when talking to you, that means the person is

   a. just a warm, touchy-feely type.
   b. expressing affection for you appropriately.
   c. indulging in inappropriate sexual behavior.
   d. coming on too strong.

18. If you notice that someone you are seeing touches *everyone* when talking to them, you think the person is

    a. just a warm, touchy-feely type.
    b. a dangerous flirt and not to be trusted.
    c. quaintly European.
    d. indulging in inappropriate sexual behavior.

19. If a person you have just begun seeing always seems to be losing things, you think:

    a. You're an absent-minded professor type with more important things to think about.
    b. You're a bit neurotic, but acceptably so.
    c. You're a few bricks short of a load.
    d. You're a real loser.

MOODS AND QUIRKS

20. If your date falls asleep during a movie, you

    a. gently nudge.
    b. let the person sleep; poor dear is probably exhausted.
    c. gently get up and walk out.

21. If your date dozes off during a movie and denies it, you

    a. let it pass.
    b. tell them to get off at the next light.

22. People can change.

    True/False

23. Given enough time, boring people can become interesting people.

    True/False

24. Given enough time, depressed people can become joyful people.

    True/False

25. Given enough time, dumb people can become smart people.

    True/False

26. Given enough time, selfish people can become giving people.

    True/False

27. Given enough time, unsensual people can become sensual people.

    True/False

28. **(Reprise)** On second consideration, people can change.

    True/False

2 Physical Attraction

Before I say anything, let's get the first question out of the way:

1. Looks don't really matter; it's only inner beauty that counts.

   True/False

   Now, if you answered "True," you can skip ahead to Chapter 3.
   But for the other 99 percent of you, the following questions can be very important. Be especially honest with yourself here, because most of us don't have a heck of a lot of control about what we find physically attractive and what we don't—it's one of those unconscious, spontaneous things that you just have to satisfy. Sure, your tastes can change as you get to know a person. But please, don't count on it.

2. **(Male Only)** I could just as easily be attracted to a flat-chested woman as to a full-figured woman.

   True/False

3. **(Female Only)** I could just as easily be attracted to a very short man as to a tall one.

   True/False

4. **(Female Only)** I could just as easily be attracted to a man with no physique to speak of as to a well-toned man.

   True/False

5. A person's eyes tell you

   a. everything you need to know about their character.
   b. how intelligent they are.
   c. how sexual they are.
   d. how much they like you.
   e. nothing much at all.

6. A sweaty person with lots of natural odor is

   a. earthy.

b. sexy.
   c. disgusting.

7. A person who pays little attention to appearances is
   a. appealingly modest.
   b. lacking in self-esteem.
   c. just a plain slob.

8. **(Female Only)** Bald and balding men are
   a. sexy.
   b. mature looking.
   c. basically unattractive.

9. It doesn't matter to me what other people think about how my date looks.

   True/False

10. When I look at someone, I automatically imagine what they will look like ten years from now.

    True/False

11. When I meet a date's father or mother, I automatically assume that is the way my date will look at that age.

    True/False

12. I don't trust a person who is basically attracted to me for my looks.

    True/False

13. **(Female Only)** You can gauge how well endowed a man is by the size of his nose.

    True/False

14. **(Male Only)** Thin-lipped women are

    a. classy looking.
    b. unsexy looking.
    c. depends on the whole package.

15. A person's weight does not matter to me in the least.

    True/False

16. If someone says to me that I look just like someone else:

    a. I hate it, even if the person I'm supposed to look like is a glamorous movie star.
    b. I love it if the person I'm supposed to look like is a glamorous movie star.

17. The most important thing I look for in a person's face is

    a. character.
    b. kindness.
    c. intelligence/wisdom.
    d. maturity/experience.
    e. sexual attractiveness.

18. **(Female Only)** Men with lots of body hair are

    a. a turn-on.

    b. a turn-off.

19. It doesn't matter to me if a person has dyed hair as long as it looks good.

    True/False

20. It doesn't matter to me if a person has had plastic surgery as long as they look good now.

    True/False

21. **(Male Only)** If a woman you are dating has a good body and wears clothes that show off her figure, you

    a. are proud to be seen with her.

    b. possessively watch other men look at her.

c. are constantly in a state of sexual excitement.
   d. all of the above.

22. **(Male Only)** If a woman really loads on the makeup, yet looks glamorous wearing it, you
   a. are proud to be seen with her.
   b. feel like there is something basically fraudulent about her appearance.

23. Aftershave lotion/perfume is
   a. a turn-on.
   b. a turn-off.
   c. depends on the fragrance.

24. The quality of a person's voice tells you a lot about
   a. character.
   b. intelligence.

c. sexuality.
   d. maturity.

25. **(Reprise, Second Consideration)** Looks don't really matter; it's inner beauty that counts.

   True/False

3 Character and Beliefs

Those two words—"character" and "beliefs"—sound kind of quaint, don't they? Retro? They're the sort of personality characteristics your grandparents used to drone on about, right?

But in my experience, it turns out that compatibility of character and beliefs count big time in a relationship. It can mean the difference between "soul mates" and "disconnects." Let's face it, when you pull your socks on in the morning, if you and that special someone don't see eye to eye on some of the basics, the prognosis for a lasting relationship is not good.

1. It is impossible for two people who are practicing radically different religions to have a long-term relationship.

   True/False

2. You can develop a long-term relationship even if one of you believes that career always comes first, relationships second.

   True/False

3. I could never seriously date a person who is always in debt.

   True/False

4. I could never seriously date a person who lies about their age.

   True/False

5. I could never seriously date a person who has racial prejudices.

   True/False

6. I could never seriously date a person who always votes Republican.

   True/False

7. I could never seriously date a person who always votes Democratic.

   True/False

CHARACTER AND BELIEFS

8. I could never seriously date a person who does not believe in God.

   True/False

9. I could never seriously date a person who *does* believe in God.

   True/False

10. You would like the person you date to

    a. be as up-front and honest as possible.
    b. give the impression of having a few skeletons in the closet.
    c. be mysterious.
    d. delay telling you really personal information until you spend a good deal of time together.
    e. delay telling you really personal information until you've got a lawyer.

11. To express your opinion to the public, you

    a. stand at the picket line shouting at the top of your lungs.
    b. march with comrades.

  c. write a piece for your local newspaper.
  d. sign a petition.
  e. sue.

12. If you run into a celebrity in a public place, you

  a. run up and ask for an autograph.
  b. smile pleasantly and move on.
  c. start pointing at the celebrity and tell everyone around you who it is.
  d. start walking alongside the celebrity so everyone will think you're friends.

13. If someone immediately starts gossiping about a person as soon as that person leaves the room, you

  a. start dishing with them.
  b. say that you don't like gossip, thank you.
  c. depends on the person being gossiped about.
  d. take charge and really start with the dirt.

CHARACTER AND BELIEFS

14. If the person you are dating is extremely self-deprecating, you think:

    a. How modest and open you are.
    b. How insecure and unconfident you are.
    c. How egocentric you are, always bringing the subject back to yourself.
    d. Depends on whether it's done with humor or self-pity.

15. If the person you are dating frequently drops the names of famous friends, you think:

    a. Wow! This person is well-connected.
    b. What a bore.
    c. How insecure they must be to have to do this.
    d. What do I have to do to meet them, too?

16. If the person you are dating frequently mentions accomplishments, you think:

    a. Wow! This person is a go-getter.
    b. What a bore.

    c. How immature and insecure they must be to have to do this.
    d. Why didn't I ever do anything with *my* life?

17. If the person you are dating never (or rarely) asks you anything about yourself, you think:

    a. Maybe they are too shy to ask.
    b. Maybe they are too polite to ask.
    c. Maybe they are too nervous to ask.
    d. Maybe they are too self-involved to ask.

18. If the person you are dating nods politely while you are talking but never really seems to be listening to you, you think:

    a. How courteous of them to even pretend to listen.
    b. What a phoney, self-involved idiot.
    c. Maybe they really are listening and *I'm* so insecure I just think they aren't.

CHARACTER AND BELIEFS

19. If the person you are dating frequently says things like, "I am on a search for my true self" and "I really have to get my act together," you think:

    a. What a deep and soulful person.
    b. Maybe we can go on this search together.
    c. How old are you?

20. I could never seriously date a person who says, "Money makes the world go around" and really means it.

    True/False

21. I could never seriously date a person who says, "Money doesn't mean anything to me" and really means it.

    True/False

22. I could never seriously date a person who says, "Love makes the world go around" and really means it.

    True/False

23. I could never seriously date a person who has more than one alcoholic drink at lunch.

    True/False

24. I could never seriously date a person who uses any kind of recreational drugs.

    True/False

25. A person who says (and believes), "We are all ultimately alone" is

    a. deeply philosophical.
    b. a lonely person who needs and deserves your love.
    c. a bad bet for a long-term relationship.
    d. full of it.

26. Rate the following personal attributes in order of their importance to you:

    a. Ambition
    b. Lovingness

c. Fairness
d. Aggressiveness

27. Rate the following personal attributes in order of their importance to you:

    a. Self-knowledge
    b. Innocence
    c. Generosity
    d. Empathy

28. The "chemistry" between two people is far more important than a "match" of personal traits.

    True/False

29. Opposites attract.

    True/False

30. Opposites may attract, but they don't make for good long-term relationships.

    True/False

4 Last Laughs—Sense of Humor

Here we go again—answer the first question and then I'll get back to you:

1. A person's sense of humor is irrelevant in a dating relationship.
   True/False

If you answered "True"—*humor is irrelevant*, move on to Chapter 5. But for the rest of us, the following questions are *très important*. Look at it this way: Statistically speaking, dating couples spend on the average ten times as much time *talking* to each other as they do *making love* to each other. (It's an energy thing.) Now while you are doing all this talking, do you want nonstop seriousness? Or do you want to have fun? A few laughs?

One person's "laugh riot" can be another person's "what's so funny?"—and a bad match here can mean a lot of hollow laughter and awkward moments that seem to last an eternity.

2. A person who can never remember a joke is

   a. like me and so what?
   b. seriously lacking a crucial personality trait.

3. A person who never seems to "get" jokes is

   a. like me and so what?
   b. seriously lacking a crucial personality trait.

4. A person who tries to tell jokes but just doesn't have the knack for it is

   a. a good sport for trying.
   b. a fool for trying.
   c. darling.

5. A person who always begins every conversation with, "Did you hear the one about . . . ?" is

   a. a bon vivant, fun to be around.
   b. an old-time boor.

6. I could never seriously date someone who didn't laugh at my wit/jokes.

   True/False

7. I could never seriously date someone who never made me laugh.

   True/False

8. If a person tells a racist joke, I

   a. laugh if it's funny (and that doesn't mean I'm prejudiced).
   b. ignore the slur, but don't laugh.
   c. say in no uncertain terms not to tell racist jokes around me.

9. If a person tells a put-down joke about women, I

   a. laugh if it's funny (political correctness takes all the fun out of humor).
   b. ignore the slur, but don't laugh.
   c. tell them in no uncertain terms that I will not tolerate jokes that put down women.

10. If a person tells a put-down joke about men, I

    a. laugh if it's funny (what the heck, it's only a guy).
    b. ignore the slur, but don't laugh.
    c. tell them in no uncertain terms that I will not tolerate jokes that put down men.

11. If a person tells a truly filthy, gross-out joke in mixed company, I

    a. laugh if it's funny—hey, that's what jokes are for.
    b. ignore it, but don't laugh.
    c. walk off in a huff.
    d. write it down.

12. If one of you thinks that the Comedy Channel is for morons and the other watches the Comedy Channel regularly:

    a. There is no hope for this relationship, best end it now.
    b. No matter, viva la difference in taste.

13. If one of you thinks that the Three Stooges are the funniest thing going and the other thinks that the Three Stooges are crude, ridiculous, unfunny, and in bad taste:

    a. There is no hope for this relationship, best end it now.
    b. No matter, viva la difference in taste.

14. Woody Allen is the funniest man alive.

    True/False

15. Eddie Murphy is the funniest man alive.

    True/False

16. *Saturday Night Live* is the funniest show on television.

    True/False

17. Martha Stewart is the funniest woman alive.

    True/False

LAST LAUGHS—SENSE OF HUMOR

18. Lily Tomlin is the funniest woman alive.

   True/False

19. Whoopi Goldberg is the funniest woman alive.

   True/False

20. If someone makes puns all the time, you think:

   a. What a wit!
   b. What a dimwit!

21. If someone cannot resist making a witty remark even if you are in the midst of a very serious conversation, you think:

   a. How refreshing! I'm much too serious.
   b. How sad! This person is obviously afraid to take anything seriously.
   c. How inappropriate! This person has no soul.

22. As a desirable trait in someone you date, how do you rate a person's sense of humor? Is it *more* or *less* important than
    a. sexual attractiveness?
    b. good character?
    c. athleticism?
    d. intelligence?
    e. net worth/income?

5 Tastes—Movies and Music

The primary dating activities have remained the same for decades: going to the movies, listening to (and dancing to) music, and eating at restaurants. We'll get to the meals in the next chapter, but for now let's get down to those Fundamental Philosophical Questions: What kind of movies do you each like? And what kind of music?

The answers to these questions may not seem earth-shaking to some of you, but consider this: What are you two going to do on a Saturday night if you've got a really bad match here?

1. A person's taste in movies is irrelevant in a dating relationship.

    True/False

2. Your idea of a great *first date* movie is

    a. a foreign film with subtitles, particularly one with a strong political message.
    b. a Hollywood thriller.

  c. an off-beat indie romance.
  d. a cult horror film.

3. Your idea of a great *second date* movie is

  a. one of your all-time favorites playing in a revival house.
  b. anything starring Brad Pitt.
  c. anything that neither of you has seen, as long as it's near your home.
  d. a cult horror film.

4. If somebody says, "I don't go to foreign movies because I hate to read subtitles," you think:

  a. How refreshingly honest!
  b. What's the matter—can't you read and watch the action at the same time?
  c. How terribly unsophisticated!

5. If your date talks to you during a movie, you

  a. engage in the conversation—your date is more important than any movie.

TASTES—MOVIES AND MUSIC

   b. ignore them, hoping they catch a clue and stop.
   c. go "Sshh!" right in their ear.
   d. go to the restroom and cry.

6. If your date eats loudly during a movie, you

   a. join in, rattling the popcorn bag loudly.
   b. ignore it.
   c. go "Sshh!" right in their ear.
   d. go to the restroom and cry.

7. If your date—without consulting you—takes you to an X-rated movie, you

   a. get into it—hey, you're no prude.
   b. go along with it, but reluctantly.
   c. declare that you don't think it's an appropriate movie and ask to go somewhere else.
   d. depends on the movie.

e. depends on your date.
f. depends on your mood.

8. Anybody who says, "I never see the same movie a second time in the same year" is
   a. reasonable.
   b. unreasonable.

9. As a general rule, Hollywood romance movies are
   a. drippy and overly sentimental.
   b. inspiring.
   c. boring.

10. As a general rule, Hollywood action/adventure movies, like *The Terminator*, are
    a. a wonderful diversion.
    b. truly exciting.
    c. dumb and unbelievable.
    d. a danger to society.

11. As a general rule, Hollywood movies about young people are

    a. amusing.
    b. so unlike true life that they're ridiculous.
    c. insightful.

12. As a general rule, there is too much nudity and sex in today's movies.

    True/False

13. As a general rule, Indies (independent movies) are

    a. way more interesting than Hollywood movies.
    b. deep.
    c. seriously pretentious.

14. There is no difference between seeing a movie on the big screen and on TV.

    True/False

15. How do you personally rate going to the movies as a leisure/cultural activity? Is it *more* or *less* important than

    a. going to a concert?
    b. doing out to dinner?
    c. reading a book?
    d. going to a museum?
    e. going out dancing?

16. A person's taste in music is irrelevant in a dating relationship.

    True/False

17. I could never seriously date anyone who thinks that rap is an art form.

    True/False

18. I could never seriously date anyone who thinks that Frank Sinatra is the greatest popular singer who ever lived.

    True/False

19. I could never seriously date anyone who thinks that grand opera is just a lot of fat ladies screeching.

    True/False

20. I could never seriously date anyone who never heard of Cassandra Wilson.

    True/False

21. Classical music is strictly for old folks and phonies.

    True/False

22. I could never seriously date anyone who never heard of Brahms.

    True/False

23. Anyone who likes classical music, but finds it hard to sit through an entire three-hour concert is

    a. refreshingly honest.
    b. copping out.
    c. uncultured.

24. I could never seriously date anyone who never heard of P. Diddy.

    True/False

25. I could never seriously date anyone who did not know the lyrics to Billie Holiday's "Strange Fruit" by heart.

    True/False

26. I could never seriously date anyone who didn't own a Mariah Carey CD.

    True/False

27. I could never seriously date anyone who could not name all the Beatles.

    True/False

28. How do you personally rate listening to music/going to concerts as a leisure/cultural activity? Is it *more* or *less* important than

    a. seeing a movie or play?
    b. going out to dinner?
    c. reading a book?
    d. going to a museum?

6 "Eat Drink Man Woman"—Food Questions

On the cover of my grandmother's cookbook is stated: "The way to a man's heart is through his stomach."

On the cover of a recent health food magazine is the claim: "You are what you eat."

Somewhere between these two extreme ideas—one *passé*, the other over-the-top—lies the undeniable fact that food plays a fundamental role in any relationship. (Yes, daters spend more time eating together than making love, but I won't go into that again.) Tastes in food and in restaurants rank right up there with movies and music, so pay attention—it's not just what comes out of a person's mouth that counts, it's also what goes into it.

1. The most sensual food is

    a. strawberries.//
    b. chocolate.//
    c. oysters.

d. whipped cream.
e. food is for eating and eating alone—it is not sensual.

2. Your idea of a romantic restaurant is

   a. a place with French menus, black-tie waiters, and no appetizer under twelve dollars.
   b. a place with checked tablecloths dotted with candle wax drippings, a waiter with a moustache that completely covers his upper lip, and twelve different kinds of spaghetti.
   c. a diner whose special for the day is *always* meatloaf, a waitress who calls you "dearie", and a jukebox with twelve different Rolling Stones selections.
   d. a country inn that has a real fireplace, a waitress with her hair in a bun, and serves twelve different kinds of squash.

3. Eating off of each other's plates is

   a. gross.
   b. an act of intimacy.

4. Feeding each other with your own forks off of your own plates is

    a. gross.
    b. an act of intimacy.

5. Feeding each other out of your mouths is

    a. gross.
    b. an act of intimacy.

6. It is impossible to have a long-lasting relationship if one of you is a vegetarian and the other is a meat-eater.

    True/False

7. It is impossible to have a long-lasting relationship if one of you is on the Atkins diet.

    True/False

8. Serving food directly out of commercial containers (e.g., pickle jar on the table) is

    a. boorish.
    b. cozy/friendly.

9. If a date invites you over for dinner and it turns out food is being delivered, you are

   a. insulted.
   b. amused.
   c. depends on what's coming.

10. If a date invites you over for dinner and you arrive to be handed an apron and are given cooking tasks to do, you

    a. are offended.
    b. consider it an expression of trust and familiarity.

11. Trying foods that you have never eaten before (e.g., hominy grits, Ethiopian porridge, blowfish sashimi) is a

    a. gastronomic adventure.
    b. gastronomic suicide.

12. Pizza "hold-the-cheese" is not pizza.

    True/False

13. The only difference between barrel-aged cheddar and Cheez Whiz is the price.

    True/False

14. Dinner out in a nice restaurant should last

    a. half an hour max.
    b. one and a half hours minimum.
    c. two hours minimum.
    d. three hours minimum.

15. Ordering three appetizers and no entree in a posh restaurant is

    a. sophisticated.
    b. gauche.

16. Talking with one's mouth full is

   a. uncouth.
   b. a sign of comfortable familiarity.

17. If your dinner date dribbles Bearnaise sauce all over, you should

   a. ignore it.
   b. quickly and casually wipe it off with your napkin.
   c. stare at it.

18. On your own personal scale of pleasurable activities, eating comes

   a. first.
   b. second.
   c. third.
   d. fourth.
   e. fifth.
   f. all of the above.

19. A person who says, "I don't deserve any dessert today" (and means it) is

    a. a highly moral person.
    b. a master of self-control.
    c. a joyless idiot.

20. Anyone who eats cold Chinese leftovers for breakfast is

    a. a lazy slob.
    b. someone who really knows how to live.
    c. someone like you.

21. You can tell more about a person by inspecting the inside of their refrigerator than by inspecting the books on their bookshelves.

    True/False

22. If you open a date's refrigerator and find open, uncovered cans of beans with greenish fuzz on top, you think:

   a. This person is an unrepentant boar.
   b. This person is in need of someone to help them.

23. If you open a date's refrigerator and find neatly stacked aluminum trays of pre-prepared meals labeled, "Monday," "Tuesday," "Wednesday," etc., you think:

   a. This person would drive me crazy in a week.
   b. This person is someone who could improve my quality of life.
   c. I wonder if this food is kosher.

24. If you open a date's refrigerator and find more beer (and other alcoholic beverages) than food, you think:

   a. Let me out of here.
   b. Poor baby.
   c. Cheers!

25. When it gets down to the nitty-gritty of either/or, it is more important to spend money on food than on (*check all that apply*):

   a. Clothes
   b. Books
   c. Beer
   d. Video rentals
   e. Toothpaste

7 Mind and Intellect

Shakespeare wrote, "Leave us not to the marriage of true minds admit impediment." He could just as well have been writing about the *dating* of true minds. Minds that truly match are a rare and wonderful thing—some call it the highest form of compatibility. And at the other extreme, minds that are truly mismatched can lead to endless misunderstandings, long pauses, and worse—boredom. To misquote Dan Quale (misquoting someone else), "A date with an incompatible mind is a terrible thing to waste."

1. A person's intelligence is irrelevant in a dating relationship.

    True/False

2. A person's books tell you everything you need to know about them.

    True/False

MIND AND INTELLECT

3. If a person does not have much formal schooling, but seems to know a lot about many things, you think:

    a. This self-educated person has learned more, in a deeper way, than someone who has had their education handed to them.
    b. What a pity this person has not had a "real" education.
    c. How am I ever going to explain this to my parents?

4. Given the choice, I would prefer being with a person who has solid common sense rather than "school smarts."

    True/False

5. Given the choice, I would prefer being with a person with a good sense of humor rather than "school smarts."

    True/False

6. I could never seriously date a person who never speaks in complete sentences.

    True/False

7. There are many different kinds of intelligence—emotional intelligence, analytic intelligence, artistic intelligence—and they are all equally valuable.

   True/False

8. Given the choice, you would prefer to date someone with

   a. high analytic intelligence (good with numbers, spelling, retention, etc.).
   b. high emotional intelligence (good self-understanding and social skills).
   c. high artistic intelligence (good sense of design and color; good taste).
   d. high abstract intelligence (good at theories and philosophical ideas).
   e. high imaginative intelligence (good at dreaming up new ideas and stories).
   f. high "quick" intelligence (good at fast and witty repartee).

9. I am more impressed by somebody who can play a mean game of chess than someone who can run the mile in under seven minutes.

   True/False

10. If you had the choice between someone who went to an Ivy League college but seems a bit on the dry side and someone who never went to college but has a wide-ranging and exciting mind, which would you chose?

    a. Ivy Leaguer
    b. exciting thinker

11. If you had the choice between someone who is more of a "thinker than doer" and someone who is more of a "doer than thinker," which would you choose?

    a. thinker
    b. doer

12. I could never seriously date a person who cannot spell common words.

    True/False

13. I could never seriously date a person who cannot do basic arithmetic.

    True/False

14. No matter how smart they seem to be, I could never seriously date a person who has not graduated from high school.

    True/False

15. No matter how smart they seem to be, I could never seriously date a person who has not graduated from college.

    True/False

16. I could never seriously date a person who has not read Kahlil Gibran's *The Prophet*.

    True/False

17. I could never seriously date a person who has not read *The Diary of Anne Frank*.

    True/False

18. I could never seriously date a person who has not read Kant's *Critique of Pure Reason*.

    True/False

19. I could never seriously date a person who does not know what the word "circumference" means.

    True/False

20. I could never seriously date a person who cannot distinguish a symphony by Beethoven from a symphony by Philip Glass.

    True/False

21. I could never seriously date a person who cannot distinguish a painting by van Gogh from a painting by Andy Warhol.

    True/False

22. I could never seriously date a person who thinks that the city Johannesburg is somewhere in Europe.

    True/False

23. I could never seriously date a person who does not read the newspaper every day.

    True/False

24. I could never seriously date a person who pronounces the "t" in "often."

    True/False

25. How do you rate intelligence in general as a desirable trait in someone you date? Is it *more* or *less* important than

    a. sexual attractiveness?
    b. good character?
    c. income?
    d. athletic ability?
    e. sense of humor?

8 Athletic Support

Ten years ago, this chapter would not have been included in a book like this one: the sporting life did not really figure in the average dater's life, especially the average *female* dater's life. But these days, many couples are just as likely to go on a roller-blading date as on a movie date, so the following questions can spell the difference between a relationship that rolls along happily and one that stumbles.

1. A person's athletic ability is irrelevant in a dating relationship.

    True/False

2. I could never seriously date someone who is a "jock."

    True/False

3. I could never seriously date someone who has never played a game of tennis.

    True/False

4. I could never seriously date someone who considers bowling their favorite sport.
   True/False

5. I could never seriously date someone who considers fishing a favorite sport.
   True/False

6. **(Female Only)** If a man will not participate in mixed-gender team sports (e.g., mixed-gender basketball, football, volleyball) because he claims he would be too afraid of injuring a girl, you think:
   a. What a considerate fellow.
   b. How brave of him to be so politically incorrect.
   c. Pig!

7. **(Female Only)** In a mixed-gender basketball game, if a man almost never passes to his female teammates, you think:
   a. This is a man who likes to win.
   b. It's just reflex, but I bet his heart is in the right place.
   c. Pig!

8. In a pick-up team game, a person who calls "foul" more than twice in a game is
   a. a stickler for fair play.
   b. a real pro.
   c. a real loser.
9. A person who jogs five or more miles a day, every day, is
   a. someone who respects the human body.
   b. someone who pushes the human body to the limits.
   c. someone with a serious obsessive-compulsive problem.
10. A person who cannot juggle *two* balls with *two* hands is
   a. a klutz.
   b. a clown.
   c. a bad bet as a sexual partner.

11. A person who thinks that anyone who is good at sports must be a little dim in the brain is

    a. cool.
    b. dim in the brain.

12. While riding with your date on a bicycle-built-for-two, you notice that your date is averaging one pedal-around for every two of yours. You think:

    a. No matter, poor dear must be exhausted.
    b. No matter, poor dear simply isn't as strong and fit as I am.
    c. What a lazy S.O.B.

13. I could never seriously date someone who would rather camp in the woods than spend the night in a luxurious hotel room.

    True/False

14. I could never seriously date someone who would rather camp in the woods *in the middle of winter* than spend the night in a *warm* hotel room.

    True/False

15. **(Female Only)** A man with a soft, unmuscled belly is

    a. cuddly.

    b. sensual.

    c. a turn-off.

16. **(Male Only)** A woman with a soft, unmuscled belly is

    a. cuddly.

    b. sensual.

    c. a turn-off.

17. **(Male Only)** I could never seriously date a woman who regularly beats me at arm-wrestling.

    True/False

18. A person who would rather work out in the gym than watch a great documentary on TV is

   a. a person with great priorities.
   b. a person with screwed-up priorities.

19. A person who is in prime physical condition is bound to be a better sex partner than a person who is out of shape.

   True/False

20. If you catch someone flexing in front of a mirror, you think:

   a. Wow, nice abs!
   b. Hey, everybody does that.
   c. Oops, this is how Narcissus got started.

21. I could never seriously date someone who couldn't do at least one chin-up.

   True/False

22. I could never seriously date someone who shows up for a dinner date in a jogging outfit.

    True/False

23. How do you rate athleticism in general as a desirable trait in someone you date? Is it *more* or *less* important than

    a. sexual attractiveness?
    b. good character?
    c. income?
    d. intelligence?
    e. sense of humor?

9 It's Just Money—or Is It?

Okay, hold your nose—I'm going to get crass now. I'm going to delve into that ultimate taboo, the subject that can make grown men blush and grown women lower their eyes. Yes, you guessed it: Money. Moolah. Greenbacks.

There are some people who insist that the very subject of money has no place in a book that is, ultimately, about affairs of the heart. And to them, I offer my sincerest apologies. But for the rest of you (Do you mind if I call you *realists*?), pay attention: The relationship you save may be your own.

1. A person's income/net worth is irrelevant in a dating relationship.

    True/False

2. A person's potential for making money is much more relevant than what is being earned now.

    True/False

3. **(Female Only)** A man who pulls out a big wad of bills every time he pays for something is

   a. a big spender—great!
   b. a big show-off—ugh!

4. **(Male Only)** A woman who always reaches for the bill in slow motion so that you are sure to beat her is

   a. striking a nice balance between "Demure Passive Woman" and "New Equal Woman."
   b. trying to have it both ways—and failing badly!
   c. basically cheap.

5. A person over twenty-one who still uses a parent's charge card is

   a. just getting started in life.
   b. spoiled.
   c. too young to have a serious relationship with.
   d. someone who can afford to have a really good time.

6. A person who regularly leaves a tip of under 15 percent is
   a. prudent.
   b. rude.
   c. European.
   d. just plain cheap.

7. A person who records every purchase in a notebook is
   a. sensible.
   b. poor.
   c. no fun.

8. People who always live beyond their means are
   a. fun for now, but a bad bet for a long-term relationship.
   b. basically irresponsible and immature.
   c. someone who really knows how to live.

9. If a person you have been dating for a month asks to borrow money, you
    a. are honored that they feel close enough to you to ask and lend it if you can afford it.
    b. are embarrassed for them, but just say that you don't think it would be a good idea and leave it at that.
    c. end the relationship right then and there.
10. If a person you have been dating for a month asks your friends or family members for money, you
    a. are honored that they feel close enough to your family and friends to ask, and urge them to lend it if they can afford it.
    b. are embarrassed, but just say that you don't think it would be a good idea and leave it at that.
    c. end the relationship right then and there.
11. Dating someone who cannot afford to do many of the things that you like to do is
    a. fine, you're flexible.

b. fine, as long as they let you pay their way when you go to the places that you want to go to.
   c. basically a drag.

12. Dating someone who cannot afford to wear presentable clothes is
    a. fine, you're flexible.
    b. fine, you're happy to supplement someone's wardrobe.
    c. basically an embarrassment.

13. Dates who always insist on going Dutch even though they clearly have more money than you do are
    a. justifiably trying to maintain equality in a relationship.
    b. cheap.

14. **(Female Only)** A man who always insists on picking up the check even though you want to go Dutch is
    a. the last of the true gentlemen.
    b. just another pig on a power trip.

15. A date who always buys you chintzy gifts is
    a. a loser.
    b. cute.
    c. a cute loser.
16. How do you rate personal net worth in general as a desirable trait in someone you date? Is it *more* or *less* important than
    a. sexual attractiveness?
    b. good character?
    c. athleticism?
    d. intelligence?
    e. sense of humor?

10 "In Dreams Begin Responsibilities"— Dreams and the Future

If ever there was a human activity that had The Future built right into it, it is dating. Going out with someone may be fun in itself, but is rarely an end in itself. Dating is a kind of compatibility test, a test for the future of your relationship. So right off the bat it is important to know the dreams, plans, hopes, and flexibility of this person with whom you are sauntering off to the movie show. Because a mistake of mismatched dreams and plans can make for a very painful future.

1. If someone you are dating dreams of becoming rich and famous, you think:
    a. Wonderful! I like someone who dreams the Big Dream.
    b. How immature! I prefer someone who is realistic.
    c. How crass! I prefer someone who dreams of doing good works.

2. If someone you are dating dreams of a life devoted to Art and doesn't give a damn about making a living, you think:

   a. Marvelous! I love a romantic idealist!
   b. Oops! This relationship is doomed.
   c. No matter.

3. If someone you are dating says, "I want to try everything there is to try in life before I die," you think:

   a. Whoopee! I want to sign on for this adventure!
   b. Big talk! I don't believe a word of it.
   c. Danger! This person is not dependable.

4. If someone you have just started dating says, "I am looking for a lifelong mate," you think:

   a. Slow down! This question should not even be on the radar yet.
   b. Great! Me too.
   c. Why are you telling me this?

5. If someone you have just started dating says, "I never want to get married," you think:

   a. No future here—goodbye and good luck!
   b. Me neither—let's just have fun!
   c. We'll see about that.

6. If a person you have just started dating says, "I have always dreamed of someone like you," you think:

   a. This is off to a very promising start.
   b. Danger! Sounds like a line to me.
   c. Danger! I can never be *real* to this person.

7. If someone you have been dating for a while dreams of living in a cottage in the country and you dream of living in a penthouse in the city, you think:

   a. No future in this—best to bail out now.
   b. Hey, it's only now that's important.
   c. Who knows! Maybe we could have two houses.

8. If someone you are dating confesses to having fantasies of three-in-a-bed sex, you think:

   a. Yikes! Let me out of here!
   b. Hmm, I have those fantasies too.
   c. What the heck—they're only fantasies.

9. If someone frequently tells you about dreams in detail, you think:

   a. Yawn! Let me out of here.
   b. Fascinating—you can tell a lot about a person from dreams.
   c. Get a life!

10. If you tell someone a vivid and meaningful dream you had the night before and that person's eyes glaze over, you think:

    a. This person is not truly interested in the real me.
    b. I know how they feel.

11. If someone says, "I never remember my dreams," you think:

    a. What a shallow person.

b. This person is in serious denial.

c. What a relief—that means I don't have to listen to any.

12. If someone tells you that they have frequent dreams about an old relationship, you think:

    a. What are they telling me this for?

    b. Who needs this?

    c. I have my work cut out for me.

13. If someone says, "I only live for the moment—the future be damned!" you think:

    a. Grow up!

    b. Wow!

14. If someone says, "I have my whole life planned out," you think:

    a. How drab!

    b. How wonderfully secure!

15. If someone says, "Life is meaningless—so it doesn't matter what you do with your life," you think:

    a. How sad for this person; maybe I can give their life meaning.
    b. What a downer! I don't want to hang around.

16. If someone says, "I believe I have a special destiny," you think:

    a. How special!
    b. How egotistical!

17. Rate the following people as having lived a "successful" life:

    a. Mother Teresa
    b. Martha Stewart
    c. Sojourner Truth
    d. Madonna
    e. your mother

18. Rate the following people as having lived a "successful" life:

    a. George Washington

b. Bon Jovi
c. Michael Jordan
d. Casanova
e. your father

19. How many children would you like to have?
    a. 0
    b. 1
    c. 2
    d. 3
    e. 4
    f. 5 or more

20. You hope to be
    a. wealthier than your parents.
    b. poorer than your parents.

c. the same.
   d. doesn't really matter.
21. You hope to be
   a. more successful than your parents.
   b. less successful than your parents.
   c. the same.
   d. doesn't really matter.

11 The Basics

I saved this chapter for the end of the "Personality Traits" section because I didn't want to scare anybody off at the start. But now that you are in good practice at this honesty business, we can tackle The Basics. These are the Big Yes-or-No's of the Dating Game. These are the questions that it's best to be clear about before you even go out on that first date—*for obvious reasons.*

1. I could date someone who is separated but not divorced.

    True/False

2. I could date someone who is married but says that they are planning to get divorced.

    True/False

3. I could date someone who is single/divorced and has children.

    True/False

4. I could date someone who is 10 years older than I am.
   True/False

5. 20 years older?
   True/False

6. I could date someone who is 10 years younger than I am.
   True/False

7. 20 years younger?
   True/False

8. I could date someone who is of a different race.
   True/False

9. I could date someone who is of a different religion.
   True/False

10. I could date someone from a different country.
    True/False

11. I could date someone who smokes.
    True/False

12. I could date someone who is a heavy drinker.
    True/False

13. I could date someone who *was* a heavy drinker but now is in recovery.
    True/False

14. I could date someone who uses recreational drugs.
    True/false

Part II
"Where Do We Go From Here?"— The Dating Experience

Okay, we've got the hard part out of the way . . . or do we? A good match of personality traits is one thing, but the dating process itself is quite another. You may be all dressed up in perfectly matching personalities, but have no place to go. This section is comprised of questions that define your desires and expectations of the dating experience itself.

And then there's that other thing—that thing we call "relationships." Again, you may have a good match of personality traits, but what if your ideas about relationships don't fit? What if your basic principles of "togetherness" are totally different? I'll tell you what—trouble. Big time trouble.

Time to face the music.

12 First Date

It's not just a "date"—it's the Big Enchilada. The night (or afternoon) that sets the tone for everything that follows—or *doesn't* follow. Not that you should be nervous (although, who isn't?), but this is the time to pay close attention—not just to the other person, but to your feelings and reactions to the other person. Any way you slice it, The First Date is The First Compatibility Test.

1. By the end of a first date I can always tell if there is any future in the relationship.

    True/False

2. The most significant piece of information you should learn about your partner by the end of your first date is

    a. why the last relationship broke up.
    b. the annual income.
    c. the favorite author.
    d. how many sex partners there have been.

3. It is important to stick to "safe" subjects on your first date, avoiding discussions of politics, religion, and sexual morality.

   True/False

4. If by the end of a first date, you think the relationship might have a future, you should
   a. say casually, "Let's do this again sometime."
   b. say sincerely, "I like you."
   c. plant a passionate kiss on the lips and say, "See ya."
   d. get the name.
   e. offer an invitation up to your place.

5. If by the end of a first date, you are sure that this relationship has *no future whatsoever*, you should
   a. say honestly, "This was fun, but I don't think we should do it again."
   b. say casually, "Let's keep in touch," but never answer the phone calls.
   c. say casually, "Would you like me to fix you up with one of my friends?"

FIRST DATE

6. I never kiss on the first date.

   True/False

7. I never have sex on the first date.

   True/False

8. The best activity for a first date is

   a. lunch—good for talk, but with a built-in time limit.
   b. dinner—good for talk and no built-in time limit.
   c. movie—no need to talk.
   d. dancing—talk optional.
   e. Other: _____

9. The most appropriate way to foot the bill on the first date is

   a. he always pays.
   b. who ever asked, pays.
   c. who ever asked, pays for the bill—and the other takes care of the tip.
   d. split it.

10. Double-dating on a first date is
    a. preferred, especially with people you know, because it takes the pressure off.
    b. to be avoided because it's hard to get to know someone this way.
    c. no preference.

11. Someone who recites their Life Story on a first date is
    a. honest and open.
    b. self-involved.
    c. efficient.
    d. a bore.

12. Anyone who carries a cellphone or beeper on a first date is
    a. a responsible person with an important job.
    b. a show-off.
    c. a killjoy.

13. Anyone who mentions a past relationship more than once on a first date is
    a. obviously not ready for a new relationship.

b. obviously asking for help in forgetting a past relationship.
   c. seriously lacking in self-control.
   d. bad mannered.

14. Anyone who keeps forgetting your name on a first date is
   a. probably just nervous.
   b. probably a little dim.
   c. probably not ready for a relationship.
   d. just absentminded.

15. If on a first date, your date automatically takes your hand when crossing the street, you
   a. pull your hand away without comment.
   b. squeeze their hand and *then* pull your hand away.
   c. hold their hand while crossing the street, then release it as soon as you get to the other side.
   d. depends entirely on how you feel about that person at that particular moment.

16. If on a first date, you hear at length about a past sex life, you
    a. say firmly but politely that you are really not interested in hearing about this now.
    b. respond by talking at length about your own past sex life.
    c. say something to embarrass them like, "Gosh, you don't strike me as the type to have had a sex life."

17. If on a first date, you find out you have been an object of a secret crush for a long time, you
    a. are flattered and say, "I'm flattered."
    b. get the creeps and say, "Don't be silly."
    c. depends entirely on how you feel about the person at that moment.

18. If on a first date you find out that you have been the object of a sexual fantasy for a long time, you
    a. are flattered and say, "I'm flattered."

b. change the subject immediately no matter what you feel.
   c. immediately say goodnight, and get the hell out of there.
   d. depends entirely on how you feel about the person at that moment.
   e. ask to hear it.

19. If on a first date, your date suddenly produces a toothbrush and goes to the restroom to brush, you think:
    a. This person has good hygiene and would make a good parent.
    b. This person is a twerp.

20. If on a first date, your date blushes frequently, you think:
    a. How sweet and refreshing.
    b. How immature.

21. I would never go out on a blind date without first checking the person's background with at least two people.

    True/False

22. I would never go out on a date with someone if I already knew that there was no future in the relationship.

    True/False

23. I would never go out on a date with someone I knew was involved with someone else.

    True/False

24. On your first date, your date shows up with a little present (e.g., flowers, a CD you said you liked): How do you react?
    a. You are put off—this is way too fast.
    b. Thrilled—how thoughtful!
    c. Embarrassed—you didn't bring a gift.

25. After your first date (where you were invited), you
    a. wait for a call.
    b. wait 3–4 days and if no one calls, you do.
    c. call the next day (if you had a good time).
    d. call that night (if you had a really good time).

13 Not Another Movie, Please!

When it comes to going out, some people have severely limited imaginations. It's either a movie or dinner or, if they get really wild and crazy, both.

But, in the immortal words of Peggy Lee, "Is that all there is?"

You can tell a lot about a person—and about your future together—by both what they *choose* to do on a date and what they are *willing* to do on a date.

1. If your date says to you, "Let's go to the seamy side of town and go bar hopping," you say:

    a. "Let's not and say we did."
    b. "Fabulous! What an adventure!"

2. If just for the heck of it, you want to take your date to the seamy side of town and go bar-hopping, and your date thinks it's a real dumb idea, you

    a. shrug and go to the movies.
    b. think, "What a drag!" and consider ending the relationship.
    c. gently urge your date to loosen up and have an adventure with you.

3. You are on your second date with someone who you kind of like, but are not sure yet. And your date says, "I'm not telling you where we're going—I want it to be a surprise." You

   a. go along happily and excitedly.
   b. ask them to guarantee that whatever it is, it's safe.
   c. say, "Sorry, I don't know you well enough for this."

4. You've been going out regularly with someone for a few months and one night your date says, "I'm not telling you where we're going—I want it to be a surprise." You

   a. go along happily and excitedly.
   b. ask them to guarantee that whatever it is, it's safe.
   c. insist on knowing where you are going before you budge.

5. You've been going out regularly with someone for a few months and one night your date says, "Just for the heck of it, let's go to a transvestite bar tonight." You

   a. go along happily and excitedly.
   b. say, "No way," and start seriously considering whether this is the right relationship for you.

6. You've been going out regularly with someone for a few months and one night your date says, "Just for the heck of it, let's go to an S&M club tonight." You

   a. go along happily and excitedly.
   b. say, "No way," and start seriously considering whether this is the right relationship for you.

7. You've been going out regularly with someone for a few months and one night your date says, "Just for the heck of it, let's go to a voodoo temple tonight." You

   a. go along happily and excitedly.
   b. say, "No way," and start seriously considering whether this is the right relationship for you.

8. You've been going out regularly with someone for a few months and one night your date says, "Just for the heck of it, let's go to a mud wrestling match tonight." You
   a. go along happily and excitedly.
   b. say, "No way," and start seriously considering whether this is the right relationship for you.

9. You've been going out regularly with someone for a few months and one night your date says, "Just for the heck of it, let's go to an opium den tonight." You
   a. go along happily and excitedly.
   b. say, "No way," and start seriously considering whether this is the right relationship for you.

10. Your idea of a romantic activity for a date is (*choose all that apply*):
    a. going to an ice cream parlor and sharing a malted.
    b. going to a street/country fair and taking a ride on the ferris wheel.
    c. going to an expensive, high-toned restaurant.
    d. going to a romantic movie.

11. Your idea of an exciting activity for a date is (*choose all that apply*):
    a. going to a roller rink.
    b. going to a play that received a rave review.
    c. going to the planetarium.

12. Your idea of a sexy activity for a date is (*choose all that apply*):
    a. going to a strip club.
    b. going to a "slow dancing" club.
    c. renting a video and staying in.

13. Someone who never wants to do anything on a date but go to the movies or go out to dinner (or both) is
    a. a bore.
    b. steady as a rock.
    c. a bore who is steady as a rock.

14 Sex

No blushing, please. After all, we've already investigated the really personal stuff—*money*! But let's be honest, sex and dating go together like, well, sex and marriage. Actually, maybe even more so. And a bad match here, for most people, is no match at all.

It may be a bit harder to be perfectly honest on this set of questions than some of the others. But do yourself a favor—dig down deep for your answers here. The long-term implications of your responses are earth-shaking—and for many of you, if the earth doesn't shake, you'll be terribly disappointed.

1. Before I commit to a long-term relationship with a person, I have to be sure that we are sexually compatible.

    True/False

2. I can tell everything of importance about a person by how they make love.

    True/False

3. I believe that it always takes time for a couple to develop true sexual compatibility.

   True/False

4. As a rule, I never have sex with a person unless
   a. I am attracted to that person.
   b. I am very attracted to that person.
   c. I am in love with that person.
   d. I am going steady with that person.
   e. I am engaged to that person.
   f. I am married to that person.

5. I could never have a relationship with someone who is bisexual.

   True/False

6. I could never have a relationship with someone who says that sex is not very important.

   True/False

7. I could never have a relationship with someone who keeps a tally of their sexual partners (assuming that number is over 5).

   True/False

8. I could never have a relationship with someone who has had sex with

   a. more than ten people.
   b. more than twenty-five people.
   c. more than one hundred people.
   d. makes no difference what the number is—who cares?

9. The best way to find out if a potential new lover is HIV negative is to

   a. ask directly.
   b. ask indirectly, like, "Gosh, did you know that some people don't even know whether they are HIV positive or not. Isn't that strange?"
   c. ask their closest friend.
   d. hire a private detective to find out for you.

10. I could never have a long-term relationship with someone who says "There are some sexual activities that I will never try."

    True/False

11. My favorite time of day to have sex is
    a. morning.
    b. afternoon.
    c. evening.
    d. night.

12. My favorite place to have sex is
    a. my bedroom.
    b. my date's bedroom.
    c. at a hotel or motel.
    d. in the backseat of the car.
    e. in an elevator.
    f. in the forest.

13. It's okay for me to have ongoing sexual relationships with more than one person at the same time as long as I have no commitment to anyone.

    True/False

14. It's okay for someone I am sleeping with to have a sexual relationship with someone else at the same time as long as we are honest about it.

    True/False

15. I could never have sex with someone who does not practice safe sex.

    True/False

16. I could never have sex with someone who insists on having unprotected sex.

    True/False

17. For me, the most important feeling in sex is
    a. the sensuality of kissing and stroking.
    b. the thrill of climax.
    c. the emotional intimacy of it all.

18. I could never have a long-term relationship with anyone who selects option **"b"** above.

    True/False

19. What percentage of time together should sex occupy in an ongoing relationship?
    a. 10 percent or less.
    b. 20 percent.
    c. 30 percent.
    d. 50 percent.
    e. 75 percent or more.

20. In order to be truly satisfying, sex should last
    a. half an hour, tops.
    b. an hour.
    c. two hours.

21. Anyone who immediately jumps into the shower after making love is
    a. wonderfully hygienic.
    b. woefully unromantic.

22. Anyone who always falls asleep immediately after making love is
    a. woefully unromantic.
    b. just tired—so what!

23. Waking you up to make love is
    a. wonderfully romantic.
    b. self-indulgent and never permitted.

24. After a few months, sex with the same person is bound to become less exciting.
    True/False

25. Sex is more important for men than it is for women.
    True/False

26. How do you rate sex and sexual compatibility in an ongoing relationship? Is it *more* or *less* important than
    a. financial compatibility?
    b. intellectual compatibility?
    c. sense of humor compatibility?
    d. political/moral compatibility?
    e. taste in music/movies/art compatibility?

15 Friends and Family

When two people join in a relationship, there are usually at least twenty other people whose lives come into contact as a result—the family and friends of the happy couple. Some call it the making of an extended family. Others call it "baggage."

How you feel about your date's family and friends is crucial. Almost as crucial as how your date feels about *your* family and friends. This whole area of a relationship can be a minefield. Proceed with caution.

1. After your fourth date, you are asked to go out with your partner's friends. You are
   a. thrilled.
   b. indifferent.
   c. apprehensive. What if you don't like them?
   d. annoyed. Those people have nothing to do with you.

2. If you meet the parents of the person you are dating and don't like them at all, you think:
   a. Oops, this is probably what the person I'm dating will be like in twenty-five years.
   b. Poor dear, such awful parents to have to survive.
3. If you meet the parents of the person you are dating and don't like them, you *say* to the person you are dating:
   a. What lovely people.
   b. Gosh, you must have had a tough time growing up.
   c. We aren't going to spend a lot of time with these people, are we?
4. If you meet the parents of the person you are dating, and it's very clear that they don't like you, you think:
   a. How can I get these people to like me?
   b. The hell with them.
   c. This relationship is not going to work.

5. If the person you are dating meets your parents and doesn't like them, you say:
    a. That's okay, as long as you like me.
    b. That's too bad, because if you don't like my parents this relationship is doomed.

6. If the person you are dating meets your dog and doesn't like your dog, you say:
    a. Goodbye.
    b. Goodbye and good luck.

7. If you introduce the person you are dating to your best (same-sex) friend, and your date proceeds to focus the attention on your friend, you think:
    a. How lovely that they get along so well.
    b. This was a serious mistake.

8. If you introduce the person you are dating to your best friend and afterward your best friend says, "That person is definitely wrong for you," you think:
    a. This is what best friends are for—to keep me from making mistakes.
    b. Hmm, I wonder if my best friend is jealous.

FRIENDS AND FAMILY

9. If you introduce the person you are dating to your best friend and afterwards your date says critically, "I never would have figured you'd have a best friend like that," you say:

   a. I guess you don't know me very well.
   b. How come? Is there something wrong with my friend?

10. If you meet your date's best friend and don't really like that person at all, you think:

    a. I wonder what this tells me about my date—nothing good, I guess.
    b. Hey, they probably just go back a long way.
    c. I hope we don't have to spend much time with this person.

11. You can tell the most about a person by meeting their

    a. parents.
    b. friends.
    c. pets.

12. If the person you are dating frequently says, "I can't see you tonight because I want to spend time with my friends," you think:

    a. Great—this is a well-rounded and loyal person.
    b. This is a bad sign—to have my date spend more time with friends than with me.
    c. I wonder if this is a cover-up for dating somebody else.

13. You tell the person you are dating that you can't see them because you want to spend time with friends, and the person you are dating says, "Hey, who's more important—me or them?" What do you say?

    a. Get used to it, my friends are important to me.
    b. You are, Darling. I'll cancel my evening with my friends.

14. If the person you are dating almost always wants friends to join you on dates, you think:

    a. Danger! This person is afraid of intimacy!
    b. What fun! I love going out in groups.

FRIENDS AND FAMILY

15. If the person you are dating does not have any close friends, you think:
    a. Danger! This person may have an intimacy problem.
    b. Wonderful! I can completely fill this person's life.

16. Rate in the order of importance in your life:
    a. Your lover.
    b. Your friends.
    c. Your parents and family.

16 WHERE PRIVATE MEETS PUBLIC

"All the world's a stage"—at least once we leave our apartments. And once we are on the public stage—be it in the street, on a bus, at a party, or in a movie theater—different styles of behavior are expected from when we are just the two of us in private.

But where do we draw the lines of what is acceptable and what is not? Disagreement on these issues can mean the difference between a happy relationship and a tense and angry one. So, *just between you and me*, pay heed to what follows.

1. It is okay to kiss—*really* kiss—in front of
    a. your close friends.
    b. strangers on the street.
    c. your parents.
    d. coworkers.
    e. none of the above.

2. It is okay to hold hands in front of
    a. your close friends.
    b. strangers on the street.
    c. your parents.
    d. coworkers.
    e. none of the above.
3. It is okay to whisper to one another in front of
    a. your close friends.
    b. strangers on the street.
    c. your parents.
    d. coworkers.
    e. none of the above.
4. It is okay to criticize each other in front of
    a. your close friends.
    b. strangers on the street.

c. your parents.
   d. coworkers.
   e. none of the above.

5. It is okay to have a real fight in front of
   a. your close friends.
   b. strangers on the street.
   c. your parents.
   d. coworkers.
   e. none of the above.

6. If you think your date is paying too much attention to someone of the opposite sex (i.e., flirting) in a public situation, you
   a. ignore it.
   b. ignore it, but chew out your date in private later.
   c. gently take your date's hand and head together to the punch bowl.
   d. start flirting flagrantly with someone else.

7. If you think your date is behaving inappropriately in a public situation—say, telling a filthy joke or taking a politically dicey position in front of people who you know will be offended—you

   a. ignore it.
   b. ignore it, but chew out your date in private later.
   c. gently take your date's hand and head together to the punch bowl.
   d. whisper in your date's ear to cool it quick.

8. When you meet your date, who is dressed inappropriately for the upcoming occasion (say, wearing combat boots to a formal dance), you

   a. ignore it.
   b. say, "Wouldn't you be comfortable in something else?"
   c. say, "I think you better change right now or we're not going anywhere."
   d. say, "Why don't we go to the movies instead?"

9. **(Male Only)** When you meet your date, who is dressed in a way-too-sexual manner for public, you
    a. ignore it.
    b. say, "Wouldn't you be comfortable in something else?"
    c. say, "I think you better change right now or we're not going anywhere."
    d. say, "Why don't we stay in instead?"
10. In a public situation, if other people gaze admiringly at your date, you
    a. feel proud.
    b. think your date must be sending out sexual signals—and it makes you mad.
    c. feel insecure.
11. If your date thinks that you are dressed inappropriately (or too sexily) for a public occasion, *but you don't think so,* you
    a. tell your date, "Tough!"
    b. change what you are wearing.

12. If you are in a public situation and your date whispers in your ear that they think you are behaving inappropriately, but you don't think so, you
    a. ignore it and keep doing or saying whatever you want.
    b. cut it short, but give your date a piece of your mind later.
    c. say out loud that your date disapproves of what you are saying but you don't give a damn.

17 THE PHONE, THE INTERNET, AND THOU

It is hard to believe that before the telephone was invented, people actually had to arrange for dates in person or by mail (or, if you were loaded, by personal messenger—*"Please wait in the salon for my reply"*). Now, not only are most dates arranged by phone, pager, or e-mail, but most of our daily conversations with someone we are dating are transmitted electronically. A high percentage of our love life is with a disembodied voice! That is why our phone habits and manners are worthy of a chapter—these constitute a major part of our relationships.

1. If after a week, a date hasn't called, your reaction is:
    a. Big deal—there are plenty of other fish in the sea.
    b. Was it something I said?
    c. The number got lost—I'll call them.

2. The appropriate way to end a phone conversation with someone you are just getting to know is:
    a. "Ummm . . . okay, well I guess I'll go."
    b. Lie. "I have call waiting and I think I should take it."
    c. "I'll let you go now."
    d. Wait until they make the move.
3. If someone you have dated more than three times does not call for an entire week (without any explanation), you
    a. call them and ask what's up.
    b. decide that it's over and get on with your life. (Who'd want to go out with such a coward anyhow?)
    c. ask a mutual friend if they know what's up.
4. If someone you are dating routinely puts you on hold, you
    a. wait patiently.

    b. hang up.

    c. inform them that you do not appreciate it.

5. If someone you are dating routinely calls you from bars or noisy parties, you

    a. are thrilled that they thought of you.

    b. are mad that they call you under such non-intimate circumstances.

6. If someone you are dating routinely calls you during your working hours, you

    a. tell them you will call back when you are not so busy.

    b. try to speed up the conversation.

    c. put your work on hold and enjoy the conversation.

7. If someone you are dating frequently calls you from a car just to shoot the breeze, you

    a. are pleased.

    b. feel like they are just using you to kill time.

8. You phone someone and they say that they are watching their favorite TV show, so they'll call you back later. You think:
   a. Hey, why not?
   b. Something is seriously wrong here.

9. If someone you have just begun dating starts e-mailing you jokes, you think:
   a. Cute.
   b. Boring.

10. If someone you have just met e-mails you to ask you out for a first date, you
    a. treat it just the way you would a phone call and e-mail back your answer.
    b. e-mail back asking them to phone.
    c. do not reply.

11. Someone you have just started dating calls you up, but after several long pauses, you realize that you have nothing to say to one another. You
    a. say, "nice talking to you" and get off the line as quickly as possible.

b. figure this is a losing situation and decline when they finally get around to asking you out.
   c. figure they just aren't a "phone person" and make nothing of it.

12. **(Male Only)** If a woman you have recently met calls you first, you think:
   a. Terrific—I love modern women.
   b. Scary—too aggressive for me.
   c. Depends on the woman.

13. If someone you have recently met calls you and you cannot remember who it is, you
   a. pretend you do remember and see how the conversation goes.
   b. say politely, "I can't place your face," and see how the conversation goes.
   c. say, "Sorry, I don't think I know you" and hang up.

14. If someone phones you and says, "You don't know me, but [Mutual Friend] gave me your name," you
   a. see how the conversation goes.

b. ask for their number and say you'll call back later, then call up your mutual friend to get the poop on this person.
c. say, "Sorry, but I don't know anything about this" and hang up.

15. If someone yawns while you are talking to them on the phone, you
    a. ignore it.
    b. say something sarcastic, like, "I hope I'm not keeping you up."
    c. hang up.

16. If someone you have recently begun dating starts talking about explicit sex on the phone, you
    a. go along with it and see where it goes.
    b. say, "I don't think we should be having this conversation," and hang up.
    c. depends on who it is.
    d. depends on your mood.

17. If someone you have recently started dating phones you and you hear another person's voice in the background, you

   a. ignore it.
   b. ask who it is.
   c. depends on whether the other voice is the same gender as you or not.

18. If somebody you have recently started dating phones after you have gone to sleep, you

   a. tell them to call back at a better time.
   b. see what's on their mind.

19. If somebody you have recently started dating phones you while you are entertaining friends, you

   a. tell them that you are busy and will call back later.
   b. excuse yourself from your friends and chat away on the phone.

20. If someone you have recently dated phones you while you are entertaining another person, you
    a. tell them that you are busy and will call back later.
    b. excuse yourself from your "in-house" date and take the phone someplace private to talk.

21. You get out of the shower and discover your phone has just stopped ringing. Do you dial *69 to see who it was and call them back?
    Yes/No

22. Someone you are just getting to know phones you and says, "I'm having a terrible anxiety attack—come over immediately." You
    a. go over immediately.
    b. try to talk them through their "attack."
    c. tell them warmly but firmly that they should seek professional help.

23. By mistake you dial someone you are dating when you really meant to phone your sister. You
    a. act as if you really intended to call them.
    b. tell them you made a mistake and hang up.
24. If a person you have started dating intends to call you on a particular night and then does not, you
    a. think nothing of it.
    b. think, one more time like that and this person is history.
    c. call to see if anything is wrong.
25. What does a person's "phone personality" tell you about them?
    a. Very little; it's what they are like in person that counts.
    b. A lot; one spends a lot of one's life on the phone in this busy world.

18 Saturday Night and Sunday Morning (and Weekend Trips)

In our busy lives, dates can be an island of fun and pleasure. And that is one reason why—given the opportunity—we extend our dates for as long as we can. Perhaps over an entire weekend.

But a two-day date with the wrong person (or even with the right person under the wrong circumstances) can be a disaster that never seems to end. It's kind of like a mini-marriage from hell. Best to be straight in your own mind about how you feel about these Saturday nights and Sunday mornings.

1. I would never go away for a weekend with someone I
    a. haven't dated for more than a month.
    b. haven't dated for more than two months.
    c. am not engaged to.
    d. the only thing that matters is how I feel about the person.

2. Your idea of a terrific Sunday morning (after an overnight Saturday date) is
   a. reading the Sunday paper in bed with coffee and bagels.
   b. catching early Mass.
   c. running five miles, followed by a sauna.
   d. making love until exhaustion.
3. Your idea of a romantic weekend is
   a. a trip to a country inn.
   b. a trip to a city where neither of you have ever been before.
   c. staying in and turning off the phone.
   d. visiting friends.
   e. visiting your family.
4. If someone invites you to go away for a weekend, you should offer to pay your way.
   True/False

5. You have gone away for the weekend with someone for the first time and suddenly you realize that this relationship is definitely not working. You
   a. say so and insist on going home.
   b. grin and bear it until the bitter end.

6. You have impulsively slept overnight with someone and when you wake up you realize you have a Sunday brunch date with someone else. You
   a. tell your new partner and leave.
   b. cancel your brunch date.
   c. don't tell your bed partner, but leave anyhow, giving a phony excuse.

7. You have impulsively slept overnight with someone and when you wake up you realize that this was not a good idea at all. You
   a. tell your new partner the truth—very gently—and leave.
   b. don't tell your new partner, but leave anyhow, giving a phony excuse.
   c. see if your feelings change as the morning progresses.

8. Someone you have just started dating invites you for the weekend to their parents' house. Do you accept?

   Yes/No/Only if you discuss the sleeping arrangements beforehand

9. Someone you have just started dating invites you to the out-of-town and overnight wedding of a friend. Do you accept?

   Yes/No/Only if you discuss the sleeping arrangements beforehand

10. Someone you have recently started dating invites you on a business trip that includes a first-class hotel and all the amenities. The only condition is, *you have to pretend you are married*. Do you accept?

    Yes/No/Only if you discuss the sleeping arrangements beforehand

11. You should only accept an invitation for a weekend trip if you are planning to sleep with that person.

    True/False

12. There is no better way to discover if a relationship has a future than by spending an entire weekend together.

    True/False

13. If you are planning to spend a weekend with someone for the first time, you tell
    a. your friends.
    b. your parents.
    c. nobody (except your roommate).

14. You are on a first date, things are really clicking, and suddenly you hear, "Let's just get in the car and go away for a few days." What are the chances of your accepting?
    a. Hey, why not?
    b. Rare, but possible.
    c. Never.

15. If you are on your first weekend-away date with someone and you seem to have run out of things to talk about by Sunday breakfast, that means
    a. the relationship won't last.
    b. we are so comfortable with each other we do not need to talk.
    c. nothing.

16. You go away to a seaside hotel on your first weekend-away date and the owner of the hotel greets your date like he is obviously a regular customer. You
    a. ignore it.
    b. ask your date casually, "Do you come here a lot?"
    c. casually ask your date, "Do you mind if we stay in a different room from the one you used on your last visit?"
    d. mutter under your breath, "Do you keep a pair of pajamas here?"

17. You are spending the night with someone and you can't sleep for the snoring. You
    a. wake them up and ask them to roll over.
    b. lie awake and say nothing.

c. slip out of bed and find another room to sleep in.

d. slip out of bed and go home.

18. You have gone away for the weekend with someone with the *explicit* understanding that you will sleep in separate rooms. Then your date registers you in the same room. You

    a. insist on separate rooms.

    b. agree to one room, but insist that there will be no physical contact.

    c. go with the flow.

19. Your idea of a romantic weekend destination is

    a. a deluxe room in a first-class hotel.

    b. a room in a motel that features heart-shaped beds, in-room Jacuzzis, and a full array of massage oils.

    c. a room in a bed and breakfast in a sleepy country village.

    d. a truck stop.

20. Someone you have grown to like very much invites you to come away for a weekend of horseback riding—but you have never ridden a horse. You
    a. accept and make the best of it.
    b. decline, saying you are not a rider and save yourself a lot of embarrassment plus sore thighs.
    c. accept, but turn up on crutches with a believable excuse that allows you to sit on the ranch porch while your date plays cowboy.

19 Fighting the Good Fight

"A relationship without fights is a relationship without passion," my Old World grandmother tells me. Is it? Or is it a sign of maturity?

Actually, that question is irrelevant in nine relationships out of ten. Because fighting—from little spats to knock-down-drag-out brawls—is simply part of the territory in the world of coupling-up. And since that is so, the frequency, quality, and rules of combat of these fights is critical in evaluating a good match.

So let the games begin.

1. If a couple fights more than once a week, their relationship is doomed.

    True/False

2. Fighting is healthy for a relationship.

    True/False

3. If something your date says really pisses you off, you should
    a. tell them so in no uncertain terms right then and there!
    b. wait until you cool down and tell them calmly what bothered you.
    c. let it pass.
    d. slap 'em in the face.

4. If a person says to you in a measured tone of voice, "I am feeling some hostility toward you," you think:
    a. What a mature way to handle feelings.
    b. What a peculiar way to handle feelings.
    c. This person has had way too much therapy.

5. How would you describe yourself as a fighter?
    a. Hot-tempered but fair.
    b. Wild and tempestuous (read: sexy).
    c. Afraid to be too aggressive.
    d. A tough match for anyone.

FIGHTING THE GOOD FIGHT

6. What kind of fighter would you like your date to be?
   a. Hot-tempered but fair.
   b. Wild and tempestuous (read: sexy).
   c. Easy to beat.
   d. A good verbal match to you.

7. Generally speaking, it is better to have a real screamfest than a civilized talk about your differences.
   True/False

8. Fighting in private is fine, but fighting in public is *never* right.
   True/False

9. If a fight gets out of control, the best thing to do is
   a. walk away.
   b. warn your partner that if this keeps going it could seriously jeopardize the whole relationship.
   c. cry.

10. Physical force is *never* permitted in a fight.

    True/False

11. Bringing up subjects that you have told your partner in utter confidence (e.g., that your mother had a secret lover) is *never* permitted in a fight.

    True/False

12. Which of the following issues qualifies as worthy of a fight?
    a. Leaving the toilet seat up for the billionth time.
    b. Being late for a date.
    c. Being rude to your mate's parents.
    d. Looking at another woman/man.
    e. Telling you frankly that your new haircut looks like crap.

13. The best part of having a good fight is
    a. getting rid of messy anger buildup.
    b. it makes you feel more alive.
    c. it breaks the boredom.
    d. making up is so sweet.
    e. the sex afterwards is fantastic.

20 To Commit or Not to Commit

Let's see, there's "We're dating" and then there's "We're seeing each other," and then, of course, there's the quaint, "We're going steady," and the ultra cool, "We're having an affair." The labels may change, but the crucial issue remains the same: *Are you two committed to one another or aren't you?* And if you are, what exactly does this commitment mean?

Clarity has never been so important. Because one person's "commitment" can be another person's "I'll see you when I see you."

1. You have been on over half a dozen dates with someone and it has been going well. Still, there hasn't really been a discussion of commitment yet. This means you:
   a. may both still date anyone you want.
   b. may both "technically" date anyone you want, but in fact *you* wouldn't, and if the other person did you would be hurt.
   c. may both heavily flirt, but not date others.
   d. are implicitly committed to each other.

2. Unless you both agree to a commitment, there is no commitment.

   True/False

3. You are seeing someone regularly. When you go away for a week or more, you are
   a. pleasantly surprised by how much you miss the person.
   b. slightly embarrassed by how much you miss the person.
   c. surprised by how little you thought about the person.

4. If you sleep with someone, that means that you are automatically committed to them.

   True/False

5. I would only sleep with someone if we were already explicitly committed to each other.

   True/False

6. I can only seriously date one person at a time.

   True/False

7. You have been seeing someone steadily for quite a while, but when you bring up the subject of "making a commitment," the other person says, "Not ready for that yet." You
   a. say, "Okay, but I'm ready when you are."
   b. say, "If you aren't ready for a commitment within the next month, this relationship is over."
   c. say, "Fine, then you won't mind my seeing other people."

8. A "commitment" in a relationship means
   a. you only date each other.
   b. you only sleep with each other.
   c. you are on your way to getting engaged.

9. There is only one real commitment and that is committing to live with one another.
   True/False

10. You are seeing someone regularly but have not made a formal commitment. Then you meet someone else who is interesting. You
    a. see this new person without mentioning it to the person you've been dating.
    b. ask the person you are dating if it is okay for you to see someone else.

11. You know that you want to commit to someone when you (*choose all that apply*):
    a. realize that you don't find anyone else attractive to you.
    b. realize that you fantasize about spending the rest of your life with this person.
    c. realize that it would break your heart if you could no longer see this person.
    d. find yourself madly jealous when you see this person talking with other people.

12. If someone you are seeing says they *never* want to get married, you say:
    a. Fine with me.
    b. That is not a real commitment.

13. Someone you are seeing says that they are getting serious and want you to date each other exclusively. You like this person, but are not ready to take that step. You

    a. say warmly, "Let's give it some more time first."
    b. say, "Okay, but I'm not sure how long this is going to last."
    c. bail out now.

14. What is the *minimum* amount of time you would have to date a person before you could make a commitment to them?

    a. One month or less.
    b. Two months.
    c. Three months.
    d. Six months.
    e. A year.

15. What is the *minimum* amount of time you would have to date a person before you could move in together?
    a. One month or less.
    b. Two months.
    c. Three months.
    d. Six months.
    e. A year.

16. Among other things, commitment means (*choose all that apply*):
    a. you pool your financial resources.
    b. you tell your friends that the two of you are an "item."
    c. you tell your parents that the two of you are an "item."
    d. you see each other every day without fail.

17. You know that you are *not* ready for a commitment if you (*choose all that apply*):
    a. still find other people quite attractive.
    b. find yourself fantasizing about other people.

    c. find you look forward to time away from the person you've been seeing.

    d. don't feel your heart go pitty-pat when you meet the person you've been seeing.

18. It is possible to commit to someone even though you know that the relationship can never last.

    True/False

19. You know that it is time to end a relationship when (*choose all that apply*):

    a. you fight more than once a week.

    b. you make love less than once a week.

    c. you find yourself making excuses for not spending time with the person.

    d. you find yourself looking around to see who else is available.

20. It is possible to fall in love at first sight.

    True/False

21. It is possible to fall in love *and* feel that this is a serious relationship at first sight.

    True/False

22. If you discover that the person you are dating has a history of lots of short-term romances, you think:

    a. Better not give away my heart too quickly with this one.
    b. Maybe I'll break the pattern.

23. If you find out that the person you are dating has recently ended a long-term relationship, you think:

    a. Beware of rebound romances—they never last.
    b. Good sign—this person likes long-term relationships.

24. If a person reaches the age of twenty-five and hasn't had a serious relationship, they are probably a lost cause.

    True/False

25. If a person reaches the age of thirty-five and hasn't had a serious relationship, they are probably a lost cause.

    True/False

21 Away Time

In today's world, most relationships are bound to have interruptions: a business project or junior year abroad takes you away from each other for the better part of a year; a vacation or business trip separates you for a week or two or three....

How do these separations figure in your relationship? Are they a good "test" of how you feel about one another? Do the "rules" of appropriate behavior change for these interruptions? Is it a good idea to plan time away from each other even if outside commitments do not force them to happen?

It's best to be real clear about these issues early on in a dating relationship. Otherwise the separations could end up being permanent.

1. You have been seeing someone steadily for several months when an exciting opportunity comes up that would take you away for six months. You

   a. jump at it no matter what your partner wishes.

    b. discuss it with your partner and only take the opportunity if your partner is fully understanding and supportive.

    c. say you'll try it for a month and see if the relationship can bear it.

2. You have been seeing someone steadily for several months when an exciting opportunity comes up that would take that person away for six months. You say:

    a. "Have a great time. I'll wait for you."

    b. "Have a great time. But I can't guarantee that I'll still be around when you get back."

    c. "Have a great time. Let's play it by ear."

3. If a person you have been seeing steadily goes away for a long time and you find yourself missing them less and less, that means

    a. the relationship couldn't have been very strong in the first place.

    b. you'd better call or write this person to tell them the embers are dying, so they'd better come back soon to fan them.

    c. you've got a life of your own and that's good.

4. If a person you have been seeing steadily goes away for a long time and you find yourself missing them so badly you are a wreck, that means
   a. this must be love!
   b. you are an insecure wimp who needs a life of your own.

5. You have been seeing someone steadily and now they have to go away for an extended period of time. During this "away" period, you both should
   a. be allowed to date other people.
   b. be allowed to sleep with other people.
   c. stay absolutely faithful to each other in every way.

6. You have been seeing someone steadily, but you usually take a vacation with your best friend. This time, the person you've been dating asks you to save your vacation time so you can go away together. You
   a. tell your friend, "sorry" and save your vacation time for your steady.
   b. tell your steady, "Sorry, but this is my life as I live it, take it or leave it."

AWAY TIME

7. You have been seeing someone steadily, but this person usually takes a vacation with a best friend. You would prefer if they saved the vacation time for you. You
   a. mention it to your steady.
   b. insist on it to your steady.
   c. do not say a word (and just feel happy that they have such a good friend).

8. The person you have been seeing steadily wants to go away for a while just to be alone. You
   a. suspect that the relationship is in trouble.
   b. act hurt and pathetic.
   c. say "Go ahead, but I can't guarantee I'll be here when you get back."
   d. think that this must be a very soulful person and respect their desire to spend time alone.

9. A relationship is strengthened by regular periods apart from one another.
   True/False

10. A relationship that cannot survive several weeks apart every year is *not* a solid relationship.

    True/False

11. A relationship that cannot survive several months apart is *not* a solid relationship.

    True/False

22 "Where Were You?"—Suspicion, Jealousy, and Trust

I have saved this set of questions for last, not because they aren't important (they are *very* important), but because they are so troublesome. Many of us manage to convince ourselves that we are beyond petty jealousies—right up until that horrendous moment when we come face to face with the green-eyed monster. If ever the expression, "To thine own self be true" applied to dating relationships, it is right here in the realm of Suspicion, Jealousy, and Trust. No, suspicion and jealousy are not pretty—they just happen to be facts of life.

1. You are out with someone you have been seeing steadily and you notice an attractive stranger is drawing more attention than you. You
    a. ignore it.
    b. *casually* say that you see what's going on and that you don't particularly appreciate it.

c. *angrily* scream that you see what's going on and you don't particularly appreciate it.
   d. start giving the eye to an attractive stranger yourself.
2. You are out with someone and you run into your date's ex. Afterward, you
   a. ask questions about the former lover.
   b. say, "What a lovely person," and leave it at that.
   c. ask, point-blank, if there are any thoughts about rekindling the romance.
3. You have dated someone two or three times and they ask you to tell them about your past relationships. You
   a. tell them—truthfully.
   b. tell them—but edit out your deepest feelings about these past relationships.
   c. say, "I'll tell you about them when I'm ready."
4. You have been dating someone steadily for a while and they never mention their past relationships. You
   a. keep waiting until they bring it up themselves.

    b. say that when they are ready, you would like to hear about their past relationships.

    c. say nothing, but start wondering if there is something unresolved going on.

5. You are dating when suddenly an old love reappears in your life and your realize you still have feelings for your ex. You

    a. see your old love secretly to discover if these feelings are real and important.

    b. honestly tell your current love that you need to find out how you feel about this old love.

    c. forget about your old love and focus on your new relationship.

6. The person that you have been dating suddenly announces that your relationship shouldn't be exclusive. You say

    a. "Okay."

    b. "Sorry."

    c. "It's been good to know ya."

7. You discover that the person you have been seeing has been seeing someone else. You

   a. make a scene.
   b. quietly explain that you know what is going on and you don't like it.
   c. say nothing about it.

8. You *suspect* that the person you have been dating is secretly seeing someone else. You

   a. say you are suspicious.
   b. do a little checking up—like calling mutual friends to see what they know.
   c. tail 'em.
   d. hire a private detective.
   e. talk yourself out of your suspicions.

9. Someone you have been dating keeps mentioning this "interesting" person of the opposite sex that they met. You
    a. feel suspicious, but do not say anything about it.
    b. feel suspicious and casually ask if they are attracted to this person.
    c. feel no suspicion at all.

10. You are with someone you have recently started dating and you see a framed photograph on the night table of someone of the opposite sex. You
    a. ask who it is.
    b. wait and see if they say who it is.
    c. "accidentally" knock it over and see if that gets them to say who it is.

11. You are in the home of someone you have been dating steadily. The phone rings, is quickly answered, and immediately hung up. You
    a. ask who it was.
    b. ignore it.

12. Someone you have been dating says you should call that night, but when you make the call there is no answer. You
    a. ask what happened later—and accept their answer.
    b. challenge the answer if it sounds fishy.
    c. don't mention it.
13. If someone you are dating starts acting jealous for no good reason, you
    a. tell them gently that they have nothing to worry about.
    b. beg them to cut it out; it's hurting the relationship.
    c. tell them if they keep acting that way, you'll give them something to really be jealous about.
14. If someone you have been dating tells you that they hate it when you look at the opposite sex, you say:
    a. "Sorry, I'll never do it again."
    b. "Lighten up, I'm only looking."

15. You discover that someone you have been dating has been checking on you with your friends about being faithful. You
    a. do not mention it.
    b. talk about other people's insecurities.
    c. get out your dump truck.

16. You discover that someone you are dating has hired a private detective to check up on your past, including your sexual history. You
    a. do not mention it.
    b. talk about other people's insecurities.
    c. get out your dump truck.

17. At the height of passion, someone you are dating calls you by someone else's name. You
    a. ignore it.
    b. give them a well-placed kick in the groin.
    c. call them by another name, too.

18. While asleep your date calls out somebody else's name. When they are awake, you
    a. ask who "X" is.
    b. ignore it.

23 THE TEST TEST

All right, I lied—I do have two more last questions.

1. Did taking *The Dating Compatibility Test* tell you a thing or two about yourself that you didn't know before?

   Yes/No

2. Did taking *The Dating Compatibility Test* tell you a thing or two about the person you are dating (or are considering dating) that you didn't completely know before?

   Yes/No

My guess—and *hope*—is that you answered both of the above questions in the affirmative. Further, I bet that if you go over your answers sometime in the near future (say, next week), you will be surprised to learn many more things about yourself and the person you are dating (or are considering dating).

The questions in this book have a way of focusing the mind and, in the process, revealing thoughts and feelings that you didn't know you had. You may have thought that you didn't have any particular expectations from dating, only to discover that you actually have some very well-defined expectations. And you may have believed that finding the right match for yourself was an impenetrable mystery, only to discover that you actually have at your disposal critical information for finding that perfect match. Now, of course, comes the Big Question: What exactly do you do with what you have learned from taking *The Dating Compatibility Test?*

Above all, you should use this information to make dating a *conscious* activity. Just going out on one mindless date after another has a way of getting tired very fast and it gets you nowhere. You may have been telling yourself that dating is simply for fun and that it doesn't mean anything beyond that, but if so, the chances are you've been kidding yourself. For the great majority of us, dating has a specific purpose: to find the right person to hook up with. It is a trial-and-error process of personal selection. And if you go about it consciously, using all the information available to you by taking the test, you will cut way down on the errors. What's more, you will soon find that you are having a more interesting time along the way.

Being conscious is one thing; being relentlessly critical is another. Use your newfound awareness gently, as a guide to finding a good match, not as hard-and-fast criteria for who "measures up" and who doesn't. Try to develop a sense of what kinds of commonalities are truly important to you and which are not. For example, is the fact that he likes his meat rare and you are a vegetarian grounds for cutting off a relationship before it even gets started? How about if she believes in capital punishment and you do not? Or you go to services daily and he's an atheist? Are all these questions of equal importance in finding a good match? Undoubtedly not. So another thing to be conscious of is your priorities.

Give all of your newfound information time to settle. Don't make any big changes in your life right after taking the test, like immediately breaking off with the person you've been seeing for the last couple of months. Just be conscious of the differences the test revealed to you. What to do next will follow quite naturally. And my guess is you are already far ahead of the game in finding the perfect match.

In the not-too-distant future, anthropologists may look back on dating as a quaint and comical ritual of an unenlightened culture. "How pointless!" they may say. "What an inefficient way of going about mating!"

But in the meantime, all I can say is that some of my happiest, most romantic and exhilarating days and nights have been spent performing this ritual. And perhaps with the addition of the *The Dating Compatibility Test*, this ritual can become a lot more efficient without losing any of its quaint and comical charm.